Contents

 World Book Inc.
a Scott Fetzer company
Chicago

What Is Childcraft— The How and Why Library?

Every day of their lives, children are busy learning. In fact, research shows that between birth and 4 years of age, a child's intellectual development is as great as it is during the years 4 to 18! In other words, the first years are as important in the learning process as those later years spent at school. And the adults around very young children are their first and most important teachers. So, one of the things children need is first-class reference material—material that is educationally sound and that children will find fascinating and enjoyable.

Childcraft has been specially developed to fulfill these needs. **Childcraft** is a multi-volume library of information. Each volume covers a separate topic, and these topics have been selected as a result of international research that has specifically identified the subjects children are likely to study at school. The educational content of **Childcraft** is presented in such an appealing way that it will hold the interest of both listeners and readers. Not only do the words and pictures hold a child's attention, but the volumes themselves are organized in the same manner in which children explore their own interests. Because of this familiar approach, **Childcraft** holds a special fascination. And when children's interests are stimulated, they learn in the most pleasurable way.

These are the four most important ways in which **Childcraft** can help your child's development:

◆ by stimulating the process of learning.
◆ by developing readiness to learn to read.
◆ by encouraging natural curiosity.
◆ by creating a love of books.

However, this does not mean that **Childcraft** is intended only for younger children. The books also have a direct appeal for older children who need high-interest, easy-to-read material. And the set itself continues to grow, because every year **Childcraft** publishes a new annual on a special topic.

Concerned adults want to do everything they can to prepare their children for school. Having good books available is a very real advantage, and **Childcraft** is a wonderful way to enrich and increase learning during the preschool and early school years.

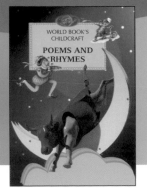

Volume 1
Poems and Rhymes

Poems and Rhymes is a collection of poems, rhymes, limericks, and proverbs. It is intended to be enjoyed by children from the early days of being read to up to the time when reading for their own enjoyment becomes second nature.

For tiny tots, there are the simple action rhymes, such as "Pat-a-cake," to which you can help them pat their hands in rhythm as you read. Rhythm appeals to all ages, especially to the very young. They'll pick up the beat of a poem long before the words. Then there are finger rhymes and counting rhymes—all great fun. And when an activity is fun, a child is learning.

A child who is beginning to read will enjoy picking out familiar words—**Childcraft** has been designed with an easy-to-read type size. And before long the same child will be reading with fluency, enjoying simple poems such as "Peter, Peter, Pumpkin-Eater."

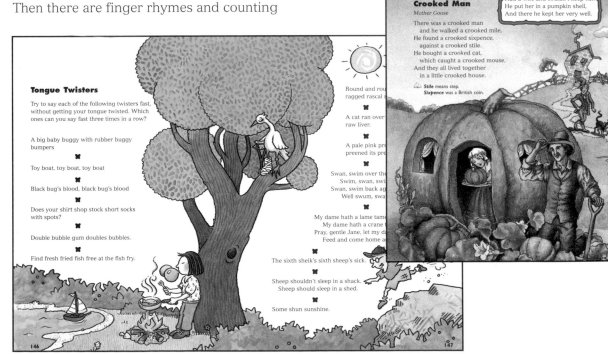

Poems and Rhymes offers a choice of reading, from nursery rhymes to alphabet rhymes, counting rhymes, and tongue twisters.

Volume 2
Once Upon a Time

Much like **Poems and Rhymes, Once Upon a Time** is a collection of readings for a wide range of ages and abilities. The illustrated stories and tales in this volume are great for reading aloud to children as well as for children to read to themselves.

Stories such as "Mother, Mother, I Want Another" have plenty of illustrations to captivate younger children and help stimulate their imaginations. And many of the stories, like "The Emperor's New Clothes," teach children important lessons.

The tales included in **Childcraft** are pulled from many different cultures. This ensures that children learn not only about their immediate world, but also about the world at large. Reading stories from other cultures promotes a child's respect for people of different backgrounds and countries.

Why the Sun and the Moon Live in the Sky

a folk tale from Africa

Long ago, Sun and Water lived together on Earth. They were great friends. Every day they danced and played together on the beach.

Sun and his wife, Moon, lived together in a warm, cheery house. The house was painted yellow, pink, and gold. Light danced all around it.

Water's house was much larger than Sun's. It was painted blue, green, and violet. A gentle wind blew all around the house, and it was very peaceful.

100

Once Upon a Time introduces children to some of the most popular legends and fairy tales, as well as exciting stories they may never see anyplace else.

Volume 3
Art Around Us

The topics in this book encourage children to learn about different forms of art and how to create art with objects they find around them. The more children learn about art in its various forms, the more they are stimulated to notice the design, color, sounds, and rhythms of everyday things.

In **Art Around Us,** young children can practice molding with clay, mixing colors, or examining textures. They can learn about ways of making sound, make simple musical instruments, and experiment with rhythms and songs. They explore many forms of theater, from opera to puppet plays, as well as costumes and makeup.

The older child is introduced to great representatives of the arts—Prokofiev, Shakespeare, Michelangelo, Ringgold, and others. Some are music-makers and craftspeople who make our daily pleasure in the arts possible.

Throughout this volume, children explore the possibilities of using odds and ends to create art. This is a book that will delight children with ways to express themselves in arts and crafts.

Getting Crafty

To do all the crafts in this chapter, you will need lots of materials. Some things you will need for only one project. But other things you will use again and again.

It is a good idea to collect the materials listed on page 13 and keep them in a large cardboard box. Then you will have the materials you need to work with.

Where will you find your materials? You may have to buy some at a craft store. But you can start your collecting at home and outside. Remember to get permission before you add something to your collection. And be careful when handling sharp objects.

Craft materials to collect
- rubber bands
- tracing paper
- bowls of different sizes
- cardboard
- clear tape
- crayons
- glue
- flowers
- leaves
- food coloring
- heavyweight and lightweight paper in different colors
- magazines
- markers
- masking tape
- newspaper
- open-weave canvas
- pencils
- pieces of cloth
- a ruler
- scissors
- streamers
- string
- tissue paper
- wax paper
- embroidery hoop
- embroidery needle
- embroidery thread

Natural objects and odds and ends are just some of the materials used in **Art Around Us** to encourage children to explore different art forms.

Volume 4
The World of Animals

The animal kingdom is one subject that has universal appeal to children. This volume introduces your children to the wonderful world of animals, their lives, and their habitats.

The World of Animals begins by explaining what makes an animal an animal and then identifies the seven main animal groups: mammals, reptiles, amphibians, birds, fish, arthropods, and mollusks. The subsequent sections then describe in detail creatures from each category. Each section is highly illustrated and shows details of the lives of the animals—where they live, what they feed on, and how they raise their young.

From the giant blue whale to microscopic paramecium, from the plodding turtle to the swift-flying eagle, The World of Animals stimulates young readers and encourages them to observe the wildlife around them.

Animals Grow Up

The seeds of a tree take root in the ground. The new tree sprouts, grows roots, and produces leaves—all by itself. Plants can take care of themselves. But, unlike plants, many animal parents must teach their young how to survive on their own.

Each baby animal grows up to live the way its parents live. It looks, acts, and sounds like animals of its own kind—and like no others.

A lion cub learns to walk and then run. It learns to eat meat. It growls and it roars. It learns to hunt other animals for food.

A baby spider grows up and does all the things spiders do. It crawls along and spins a sticky web that will catch insects to eat.

A young parrot learns to fly. It knows how to crack nuts and seeds with its bill. It squawks and whistles like other parrots.

The baby penguin will grow to look just like its parent.

Most polar bear cubs live with their mother for their first two years.

Every animal learns to live like the other animals of its kind. Each animal does what it must do to stay alive. That's the way of the animal world.

A mother camel watches over her calf until it i ready to take care of itself.

16

The World of Animals studies many aspects of the animal kingdom, from what an animal is to how animals grow up, and more.

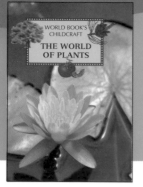

Volume 5
The World of Plants

This volume lets children tour **The World of Plants**—a fascinating trip! With a skillful combination of exquisite illustrations and photography, this volume explores the wonders and mysteries of the plant world.

The natural world often prompts children to ask the most difficult questions, such as "Why are leaves green?" or "What's inside a seed?" The answers to these and many other questions are inside this volume.

In addition to the facts of plant life, children learn how important plants are to people—how people use them for food and to make paper, cloth, even buildings and medicine. The text also shows how important it is that everyone, in turn, look after the world of plants.

Colorful illustrations are used throughout **The World of Plants** to simplify concepts for children.

Volume 6
Our Earth

This book for young children is an introduction to the fascinating earth sciences. The volume approaches the subjects process by process, describing each topic in a strongly visual manner. For example, in the volcano section, simple, clear diagrams accompany the text, alongside action photographs of eruptions and formations.

Children are always full of questions about the world about them, such as: "Where does the water in a river go?" "Where does rain come from?" and "Why is the sunset red?" In this volume, you can find simple explanations for these and many other mysteries, ranging from thunderstorms and earthquakes to snowflakes and glaciers.

Our Earth describes the dramatic phenomena of the earth's activities and stimulates children's interest in their own environment.

A spring gushes out of the rocks and joins the river below.

spring

tributary

Where Rivers Begin and End

High on a mountain, snow melts. Some of the melted snow trickles down the mountainside, finding the easiest path. It is so narrow you could step across it.

Another trickle of water bubbles out from under a rock from underground water called a spring. This trickle joins the melted snow, making a wider, faster-moving stream. It flows down the

mountain increasing speed. More streams, or **tributaries**, come together to form a river.

Soil and stones, carried along by the rushing water year after year, cut a groove into the mountainside. The bottom of this groove is the bed of the river. The high sides of the groove are its banks.

The rushing river hurries to the edge of a cliff in the mountainside and falls in a roaring, tumbling, splashing waterfall.

In a steep place near the bottom of the mountain, the fast-moving river has worn away the soft rock. Only bumps of hard rock are left sticking up as the river swirls and foams around them. This part of the river is called the rapids.

The Niagara River rushes over a cliff, forming Horseshoe Falls between the United States and Canada.

It has a head at one end and a mouth at the other end. What is it? It's a river! The head is where the river begins. The mouth is where the river ends.

waterfall

rapids

84

85

In **Our Earth**, clear diagrams are used to complement dramatic photos.

Volume 7
The Universe

What's the difference between a star, a planet, and a moon? Is there such a thing as a shooting star? Or a black hole in space?

In this book about astronomy, our own planet is described in the context of the solar system. Each planet is also dealt with in detail. Then comes an awe-inspiring journey out beyond the confines of our own solar system— to find out how people study space and to glimpse the galaxies of the universe, where great stars are even now in the process of being born or slowly dying.

In addition to astronomy, children become acquainted with space technology and research in communications. Leading figures in astronomy—past and present—and a photo essay of a shuttle mission are also featured. Galaxies, comets, constellations, and much more in **The Universe** will make any child interested in space.

Big photos throughout **The Universe** give children a close-up view of objects in space.

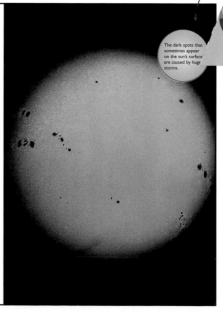

The dark spots that sometimes appear on the sun's surface are caused by huge storms.

The Sun Has Chickenpox!

Have you ever had chickenpox? If you have, you probably remember that parts of your body were covered with spots. Scientists who study the sun say that sometimes it looks as if the sun has chickenpox, too!

But the sun's dark spots, called **sunspots**, are not caused by a virus the way chickenpox is. Sunspots are caused by giant storms on the sun's surface. From Earth, these storms look like dark dots because they are much cooler than the rest of the sun's blazing hot surface.

Most sunspots start off in pairs and drift apart. Because they are so far away from us, they look small. But just one of these spots is bigger than the whole Earth!

Sunspots do not occur all the time. Sometimes, the sun's surface is covered with them. Years later, there may be very few. Scientists have learned that they run in **cycles** of about 11 years.

This picture was taken through a special camera that is able to show the cooler spots on the sun's surface. The yellow and red areas are sunspots.

34

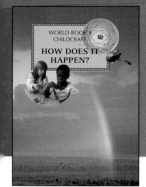

How Does It Happen?

Children are introduced to basic principles of science in this volume. Simple text and generous illustrations help children understand the interaction of matter and energy in the world around them.

The material in **How Does It Happen?** gives children a solid grounding in the basics of machines, movement, kinds of matter, sources of energy, heat and cold, light, sound, and electricity. Each engaging subject is explained in simple terms and illustrations.

Children can use the book to satisfy their curiosity about everyday things—how magnets work, what condensation is, how an airplane stays up in the air, and how electricity can be switched on and off. With their newfound knowledge of the principles, children are then invited to try simple experiments.

High and Low

When you ring a small bell, it vibrates quickly, making a high ringing sound.

Zzzeee goes the tiny mosquito as it zips past your ear. VROOOM growls a big tractor as it rumbles past you. The sound the mosquito makes is much higher than the sound of the tractor. Why are the sounds different?

When something vibrates, sound travels outward from it in waves. Each vibration—each complete back-and-forth motion—makes a single sound wave. The faster something vibrates, the more sound waves it makes and the higher the pitch.

A mosquito makes high-pitched sounds because its wings vibrate very fast—about a thousand times a second!

A tractor makes low-pitched sounds because its heavy metal parts vibrate slowly. The slow vibrations make only a few sound waves every second—the low rumble that you hear.

When you ring a large bell, it vibrates more slowly, making a lower ringing sound.

148

149

How Does It Happen? aims to explain complicated ideas in simple, familiar terms, using examples that children will understand from their lives.

Volume 9
How Things Work

How does a refrigerator make things cold? How does a picture appear on a television screen? What makes a car work?

How Things Work answers these questions and many more, applying the concepts discussed in **How Does It Happen?** to the everyday world. The article "Why Things Float" gives a very clear and practical demonstration of the principle of water displacement. In addition to helping children understand how things function, this volume also underlines the value of raw materials. "From Ore to Metal" explains the importance of metals, where they are found, and how they are obtained from their ores.

By dipping into **How Things Work**, children gain a greater appreciation of the application of the principles of science and the importance of technology in our everyday lives.

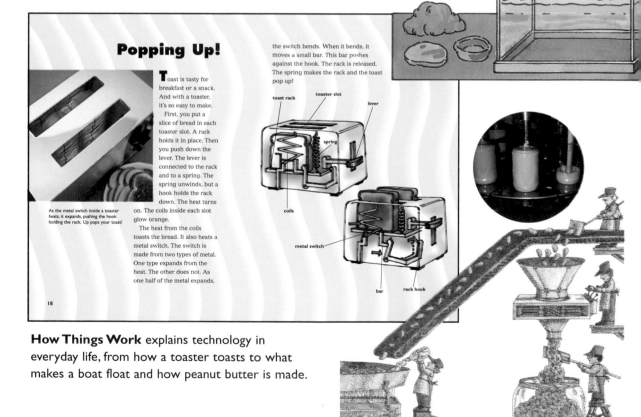

Popping Up!

Toast is tasty for breakfast or a snack. And with a toaster, it's so easy to make.

First, you put a slice of bread in each toaster slot. A rack holds it in place. Then you push down the lever. The lever is connected to the rack and to a spring. The spring unwinds, but a hook holds the rack down. The heat turns on. The coils inside each slot glow orange.

The heat from the coils toasts the bread. It also heats a metal switch. The switch is made from two types of metal. One type expands from the heat. The other does not. As one half of the metal expands, the switch bends. When it bends, it moves a small bar. This bar pushes against the hook. The rack is released. The spring makes the rack and the toast pop up!

As the metal switch inside a toaster heats, it expands, pushing the hook holding the rack. Up pops your toast!

toast rack

toaster slot

lever

spring

coils

metal switch

bar

rack hook

18

How Things Work explains technology in everyday life, from how a toaster toasts to what makes a boat float and how peanut butter is made.

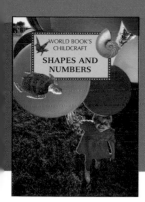

Shapes and Numbers

ere's a book that can demonstrate that mathematics is really fun! **Shapes and Numbers** is filled with puzzles, stories, and surprising facts that show easy logical relationships in numbers and shapes.

"Inventing Numerals" explains how the first numerals came to be, while "Other Ways to Count" explains the differences among the counting systems of many countries. And, of course, this fascinating historical background is enhanced by clear, inventive illustrations.

There are many surprises in **Shapes and Numbers**. Children can learn the importance of zero, or they can delve into the mysteries of calculator games and magic squares.

Inventing Numerals

Once people began to count, how did they remember the numbers they had counted? They needed a way to write down the numbers—so they invented **numerals**. Numerals are symbols that stand for numbers.

Some of the first numerals were invented by the Egyptians about 5,000 years ago. Their marks for the first nine numbers look like pictures of fingers.

The Egyptians had special symbols for the numbers 10, 100, 1,000, 10,000, and 100,000. A picture of a lotus flower was the numeral for one thousand. There were thousands of lotus flowers in Egypt's Nile River. So the Egyptians probably thought a lotus was a good symbol for a big number like 1,000.

The numeral for one hundred thousand was a picture of a tadpole. Lots and lots of frogs lived along the Nile River. When their eggs hatched, the water must have been full of tadpoles. That may be why the Egyptians used the tadpole as their symbol for a huge number like 100,000.

1,000

100,000

56

57

The text and illustrations of **Shapes and Numbers** can help make learning mathematical concepts an enjoyable experience.

Volume 11
About You

Throughout the pages of this book, a child can get to know another subject that holds a particular fascination—human biology.

Starting with the outside—the part that everyone sees—**About You** describes how each part of the human body works and explains the relationship between the various parts of the body and the brain.

About You explains a particularly complex subject in simple language and uses illustrations to highlight and further clarify the text. For example, "One You, Two Sides" has children experiment with a mirror and a photo to see how the halves of the body are different.

In addition to the structure of the human body, **About You** also describes a physical and emotional process that is fascinating to all children—growing up and maturing.

One You, Two Sides

Your head has two sides, a right side and a left side. Each side has an eye, a cheek, an eyebrow, an ear, and a nostril. So, do both sides look the same? Take a closer look and see.

Look at yourself in a mirror.

Are your eyebrows exactly alike? Or is one more curved than the other?

Are your ears in exactly the same place on each side of your head? Do they have the same shape?

Does your nose have the same shape on both sides?

What about your hair? Does it look the same on both sides?

Do your eyes have the same shape?

In these pictures, one side of the girl's face has been exactly copied to make the other side. Does the girl look the same in both pictures?

This half was copied.

This half was copied.

Now you can probably see that each side of your face is a bit different. This is okay. Everyone has two different sides.

Other parts of your body do not match exactly, either. Look at your hands. Is one bigger than the other? How about your feet? Do the toes on each foot have different shapes?

TRY THIS

What if the two sides of your face were exactly alike? What would you look like? Try this and see. Find a photo of yourself. Hold a mirror along the nose as shown here. Does the new "picture" of you look like you? Turn the mirror around and look at the other half. Does this "picture" look the same as the first one!

13

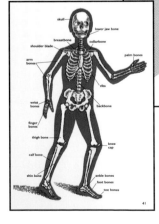

skull
lower jaw bone
breastbone
collarbone
shoulder blade
palm bones
arm bones
ribs
wrist bones
backbone
finger bones
thigh bone
knee cap
calf bone
ankle bones
shin bone
foot bones
toe bones

41

Simple illustrations and text in **About You** help children to understand basic scientific principles.

Volume 12
Who We Are

This book explores the people and cultures of many nations. Throughout the book, children learn that the peoples of the world are alike in many ways and different in many others.

Who We Are describes our different beliefs and customs. We grow and prepare different kinds of food. Clothing differs from country to country, and our homes may be anything from a portable tent to a concrete skyscraper.

But the fact remains that we all share common needs. We all need love and friendship, food and shelter.

In a shrinking world, we're learning to live alongside each other, to share languages, customs, and each other's values. The children of today will be truly international citizens with, hopefully, all the tolerance and understanding that implies.

Pages from **Who We Are** focus on different cultures around the world.

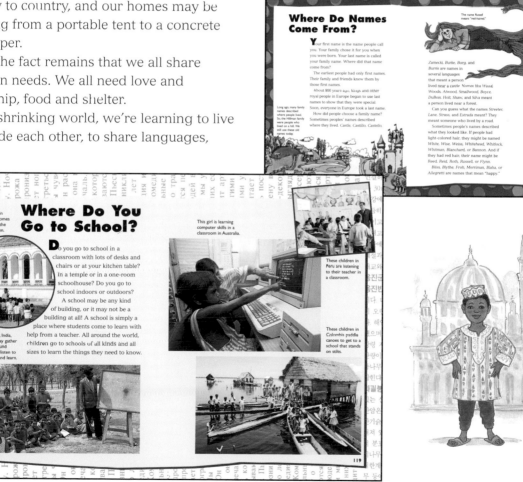

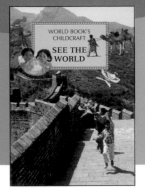

Volume 13
See the World

See the World is a child's first geography book. It introduces children to the earth's continents and to important and famous sites around the world. This volume even tackles the basics of housing, transportation, maps and mapmaking.

This book shows the ways people live in different climates. Along with showing how geographically far apart different peoples are, **See the World** shows how transportation and technology have brought everyone closer together.

In addition, this volume introduces children to some of the most famous places in the world. Readers visit castles, national governments and monuments, ancient wonders, natural wonders, and famous skyscrapers, along with many other well-known places. These places are shown in bright illustrations and photographs designed to captivate a child's imagination.

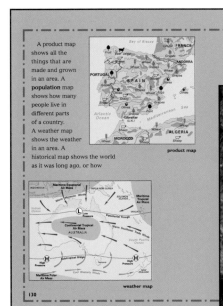

A product map shows all the things that are made and grown in an area. A **population** map shows how many people live in different parts of a country. A weather map shows the weather in an area. A historical map shows the world as it was long ago, or how

product map

weather map

130

See the World gives children tours of exciting places, a close-up view of how people live and travel, and a guide to using maps.

What Are Castles?

Some of the world's most amazing buildings were built for protection, not

The famous French author Michel de Montaigne lived his whole life in this castle.

beauty. Hundreds of years ago, people in different parts of the world had many rulers. The rulers often fought each other. Powerful rulers built castles to live in with

their family, helpers, priests, soldiers—and farm animals!

Many of the castles were made of stone. Often they were built around an open courtyard. They had high walls that could be 30 feet (10 meters) thick to protect against enemies. Some castles had towers at each corner.

Sometimes the walls were surrounded with deep, wide ditches that were usually filled with water. These were called moats. To protect the castle, guards looked out from the towers and walked along the tops of the walls. They hid behind stone fences called battlements and shot arrows at attackers. When visitors came, the guards would lower a drawbridge so people could walk or ride across the moat. Then the visitors would have to pass a gatehouse.

Inside, there was a large great room where people met and ate meals. A huge fire in the fireplace took away the chill. So did tapestries, or hanging cloths, placed around the castle walls. People spread sweet-smelling plants on the floors and changed them every month.

The king slept in the bedroom in the Linde Palace in Bavaria, Ger

86

Volume 14
Celebrate!

In this book, children learn how people celebrate all over the world and discover that on almost every day of the year, there is a celebration somewhere in the world.

Many celebrations center around natural events, such as the full moon or the longest day of the year. Sometimes the very different ways people celebrate the same event are fascinating; other times, the similarities among celebrations, even in far distant places, are even more interesting.

Using **Celebrate!**, a child can answer the question "Who shares my birthday?" by looking up the date of his or her birth to find what famous historical figures were born on the same date.

Celebrate! gives a brief history of holidays around the world.

These children are dressed in Greece in traditional clothes for an Easter celebration. Easter is a religious holiday. It is also a "floating holiday" that is always on a Sunday.

The Chinese calendar

The Chinese calendar follows the moon. But it also groups years into sets of 12. Each year is named for an animal. The first of the twelve years is the Year of the Rat. This is followed by the years of the ox, tiger, hare, dragon, snake, horse, sheep, monkey, rooster, dog, and pig.

Each year on the Chinese calendar is named for an animal.

rat   ox
pig   tiger
dog
rooster   hare
dragon

Holidays and Calendars

Some holidays follow calendars based on the moon. These days are called "floating holidays" because they float around on our standard calendar. They are not celebrated on the same day each year. Many of these floating holidays are religious. They follow a religious calendar.

16

Dolls used in the Girls' Festival represent Japan's **emperor** and empress and members of their court.

Doll Festivals

Does your family have special dolls that decorate the shelves or mantel? In Japan, people display special sets of dolls every year on March 3 and May 5. These are doll festival days. The one on March 3 is the Girls' Festival, and the one on May 5 is the Boys' Festival.

During these celebrations, families display dolls that have been handed down for generations. Through the dolls, the children learn about their country's culture, history, and outstanding men and women.

March 3 May 5

60

St. Patrick's Day

March 17

In Dublin, Ireland, people wear **shamrocks**. In Chicago, the river is dyed green. It's St. Patrick's Day, a good time to wear a bit of green and enjoy Irish **traditions**.

The color green is a reminder of the beautiful green countryside of Ireland. It is also the color of the shamrock, the cloverlike plant that is the national symbol of Ireland.

In Ireland, St. Patrick's Day is a holy day. People attend religious services. Saint Patrick, Ireland's **patron saint**, brought Christianity to Ireland. In many U.S. and Canadian cities, people celebrate with parades and enjoy Irish music and foods. In New York City, more than a hundred bands and a hundred thousand marchers join in the St. Patrick's Day parade along Fifth Avenue. The parade lasts for hours.

61

Volume 15
Guide and Index

In the same way that the other volumes of **Childcraft** will help your child understand and learn about the modern world, this volume is designed to help you understand and enjoy the challenge of caring for children.

The first section, "Learning with Childcraft," helps you become familiar with the books and the material presented in them so that you can be the best teacher for the children in your life. It helps you use the set to its full potential.

The second section, "Growth and Development," helps you understand your young student and provides guidelines for solving some of the problems that arise at each stage of development. A series of articles, "For Special Consideration," helps you with issues such as traveling with young children and helping a child with learning disabilities.

The final section of this volume contains the complete index for the **Childcraft** set.

Children, Television, and the Internet

Television affects the way children spend their time and what and how they learn. Many children also spend time playing video games and using the Internet. Are these activities safe for children? What can parents do to control the influence of these activities?

Watching television

Television provides people with a wide range of new experiences. Without leaving their homes, TV viewers can see how people in far-off lands look and live. They can glimpse real-life tragedies and moments of great triumph.

While there is little agreement about how television specifically affects young people, it clearly has an impact on them. Young children, who learn by observing, will try out some of the behaviors they see on TV, both positive and negative. For this reason, children who watch programs with violent overtones tend to behave more aggressively. Children also may be influenced by the sexual behavior they see on television, adopting it at a far earlier age than their parents want.

Many social scientists believe that young people also likely form false impressions from watching a lot of television. They may come to believe in the stereotypes they see and form prejudices, or they may

be disappointed in their own less-than-idyllic family life. Television rarely shows the effort that goes into successful lives, so children may not understand that success generally comes through hard work and sacrifice. It also does not help them understand the consequences of actions, including violent acts.

Aside from leaving people with unrealistic impressions, television viewing takes time from important leisure activities, such as reading, conversation, social gatherings, and exercise. Ads for products also influence children, increasing their desires for material goods.

Living with television

Parents can do a great deal to control the influence of TV on children's lives:

- Limit the amount of television children watch each day. Children need to learn that watching TV is a privilege; it is not a right.
- Forbid children to watch violent and overly sexual programming.
- Avoid using television as an electronic baby sitter. Instead parents should look for other ways to engage their children if they are busy.
- Watch television with children and take the opportunity to teach them about what they see.

Like TV watching, Internet use needs safe limits and guidance from parents.

Parents can also avoid watching a lot of television themselves. By being good role models, they can diminish television's importance in family life. It is worth the effort!

Using the Internet

The Internet is a vast computer network that connects many of the world's businesses, institutions, and people. It has made huge amounts of information accessible to more people than ever before.

While the Internet is a great tool, there are questions about children's use of it. Not all information on the Internet is accurate, and some is deliberately misleading. Many parents are concerned about violent or pornographic material. They worry about possible criminals lurking in "chat rooms," through which people send messages to each other, and seeking to arrange face-to-face meetings with unsuspecting victims.

Living with the Internet

Just as parents have rules about watching TV, it is important to have rules about using the Internet. To keep children's time on the Internet safe, productive, and fun, parents should follow these guidelines:

- Set limits on the amount of time children can spend online each day or each week.
- Do not let "surfing" the Internet take the place of homework, outdoor play, or friends.
- Make sure children know that people online are not always who they say they are and that online information is not necessarily private.
- Teach children to never give out personal information, never use a credit card online without permission, never share passwords, never arrange a face-to-face meeting, never respond to messages that make them feel confused or uncomfortable, and never use bad language or send mean messages online.
- Make a point of participating in children's online time. Stay involved and monitor what children are doing online.

Special programs known as parental control software can help parents block access to sites that may be unsuitable for children. Education associations, Internet providers, and libraries often have information on blocking software.

94

95

Why Is Childcraft Special?

Its philosophy

Childcraft is for children. This is a statement that represents the essence of **Childcraft's** philosophy. **Childcraft** deals with subjects that stimulate children's natural curiosity. It provides answers to many of their questions and expands their horizons.

Its international message

One of the important aims of **Childcraft** is to foster in children an understanding of their roles as international citizens. Articles on world problems such as urban overcrowding or environmental issues such as pollution and recycling address topics that today's child hears about in school or on television.

At a personal level, the child can be encouraged to appreciate and accept differences in religion, skin color, or physical ability that make everyone special and to understand that all people are part of a world family.

How Can People Protect the Earth?

For thousands of years, people have used the earth's land, water, and air. Also, people have also polluted the earth with their waste, harmful chemicals, and other poisons.

Now people all over the world are working to protect the earth. They are working to preserve land, stop **pollution**, save natural **resources**, and protect endangered wildlife. There are many ways to help the earth. You can help, too.

170

Its language

The text of **Childcraft** aims to speak directly to the young listener or reader. The objective is to first capture the imagination and then expand on a topic in a clear and interesting way.

Young children love the sounds that certain words make, just as they love sentences that have rhythm. They also love to learn and use new and sometimes difficult-sounding words.

So, whenever it's necessary to introduce a specialized word, the text is written in such a way that the meaning of the word is explained.

As every caregiver knows, the questions children ask can't always be answered in simple words. Nevertheless, the **Childcraft** writers, while keeping the language simple, provide easy explanations of complex ideas.

Its features

Childcraft has many features to help children navigate through its chapters. The boxes marked **Know It All!** have fun-filled facts. Children can amaze their friends with all that they learn.

The books also have many activities that children can do at home. Look for the words **Try This!** over a colored ball. The activity that follows offers a hands-on way to learn more about the subject of the book. For example, in **The Universe**, children can make a hanging model of the planets in the solar system.

Each activity has a number. Activities with a 1 in a green ball are simplest to do. Those with a 2 in a yellow ball may require a little adult help with tasks such as cutting or measuring or using hot water. Activities with a 3 in a red ball may need more adult help.

A Try This! activity that has a colorful, geometric border around its entire page is a little more complex or requires a few more materials. Children should take a moment to read through the step-by-step instructions and to gather any materials needed before they begin.

Some words are printed in bold type, **like this**. These are words that might be new to children. They can find the meanings and pronunciations of these words in the **Glossary** at the back of the book. They can turn to the **Index** to look up page numbers of subjects that particularly interest them.

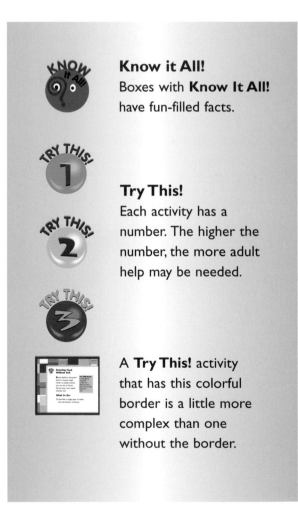

Know it All!
Boxes with **Know It All!** have fun-filled facts.

Try This!
Each activity has a number. The higher the number, the more adult help may be needed.

A **Try This!** activity that has this colorful border is a little more complex than one without the border.

Mammals in the Sea

Most kinds of mammals live on land. But seals, whales, and a few other mammals live in the sea. They can stay underwater for a long time, but these mammals breathe air through their lungs. They rise above the water to breathe.

Whales look so much like **fish** that many people think they are fish. But they are mammals. They have hair, they are warm-blooded, and their babies drink mother's milk. Dolphins and porpoises are small whales.

Seals, sea lions, and walruses are mammals that spend much of

Elephant seals spend much of their time in the water, but they breathe with lungs like other mammals.

Killer whales are mammals that live in the ocean. This 3-day-old killer whale is drinking milk from its mother.

KNOW It All Dolphins and porpoises belong to the same family, but they are not the same animal. How can you tell the difference between a dolphin and a porpoise? A dolphin has a pointy snout, cone-shaped teeth, and a sharply sloping forehead. A porpoise has a rounded snout, flat teeth, and a gently sloping forehead. Also, porpoises are smaller than dolphins.

dolphin

porpoise

their time in the water and some time on land. When they come onto land, they waddle about on their fins.

Another group of sea mammals includes dugongs and manatees, which are sometimes called sea cows. These animals look a bit like walruses without tusks. Instead of hind flippers, each of these animals has a wide, flattened tail.

dugong

manatee

Its art and design

It is important to write about things that interest young children and to present that content in exciting and informative language. But something else is needed to ensure that content and approach work together.

In **Childcraft**, that something else is the design. The illustrations are a very important part of **Childcraft**—more than half of each two-page spread is devoted to either photographs or specially commissioned art. These illustrations are used to inform. Even when children are too young to read the words, they can learn a great deal from looking at the pictures, such as the superb wildlife photos.

Good art and design in themselves can stimulate and develop interest, and striking illustrations often make a lasting impression on children. In **Childcraft**, hundreds of full-color illustrations bring each topic to life and neatly explain many difficult concepts.

Growing Up with Childcraft

Intellectual development

A child is a bundle of curiosity about practically everything. Early guidance and a daily life rich in varied fun, educational experiences, and activities greatly help to stimulate natural intelligence, creativity, and fine motor skills. **Childcraft** offers firsthand help by providing materials with high motivational content presented in such a way that children can use and understand them at an early age.

Physical development

Each person grows according to a unique plan—a combination of heredity and environment. But, of course, there's a great deal more to growing up than getting enough exercise and sleep and eating a nutritionally sound diet. Children should be encouraged to learn more about their bodies, to understand exactly what physical development means. **About You** explains what takes place in the process of physical growth and development. It helps children understand the changes they are experiencing.

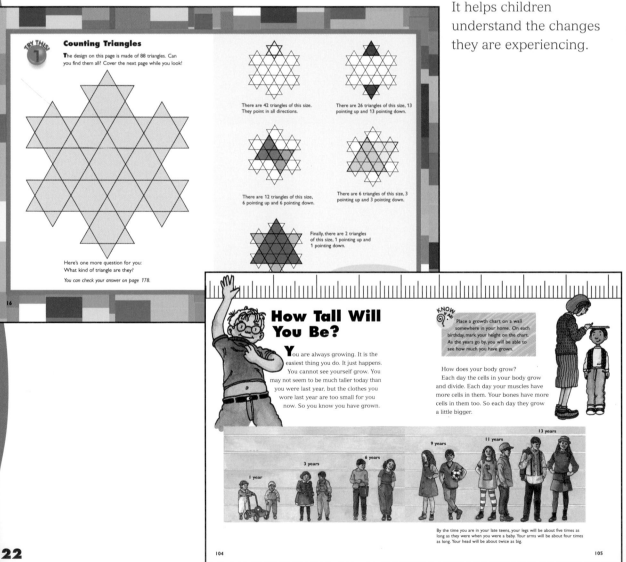

Emotional development

Sound emotional development is related to every other aspect of a child's development. It's a continuing process, taking place at home, in the classroom, and at play. **Childcraft** contributes to the process by showing children how people express their emotions. **About You** deals with emotional development and shows how emotions such as happiness, sadness, love, anger, and fear affect our actions.

Art Around Us offers examples of how a work of art often reflects the emotions of its creator. Throughout **Poems and Rhymes** and **Once Upon a Time**, children see characters experiencing and expressing emotions in various circumstances.

Many other features in **Childcraft** provide a similar insight into a young reader's own emotions.

Sometimes you feel angry at your brothers and sisters.

sad because your friend seems to like someone else better.

Understanding how and why your feelings change is part of growing up. Sometimes feelings can be very confusing.

Not all feelings are good, but it is still okay to have them. It is also okay to let people know how you feel—and why you feel that way. But it is not okay to do whatever your feelings make you feel like doing. It is not okay to hit someone or call someone a name because you are angry.

How do you think this boy is feeling? How is he telling you how he feels?

Your Ever-Changing Feelings

Have you ever noticed how quickly your feelings can change? One day you might feel happy because you made a new friend. The next day you might feel

You tell people how you are feeling in many ways. You tell them with your words, your face, and what you do with your body. When you are angry you might want to frown, make a fist, or yell. But you might find it more helpful to talk.

If your feelings upset you, talk to someone you trust. You will learn that everyone feels the same way you do, at some time or another.

Playing with your friends can make you happy.

Moral development

The world can seem a confusing place to children. They meet with new ideas, values, and philosophies nearly every day. Children need to develop standards that will help them distinguish right from wrong. These standards are, of course, set by the adults the child comes in contact with.

But it's important not to underestimate the strong influence that reading can have. Children can find in **Childcraft** examples of healthy moral values that can reinforce and strengthen a responsible attitude.

In the pages of **Childcraft**, children see people both as individuals and as part of society. They can find examples from many different societies demonstrating how people work together for a common goal and especially how people work to help others.

The world can seem a confusing place to children. They meet with new ideas, values, and philosophies nearly every day. Children need to develop standards that will help them distinguish right from wrong. These standards are, of course, set by the adults the child comes in contact with.

Social development

A child's social development starts right after birth. Then begins the lifelong adventure of being an individual—and also being a social creature who depends on others and is depended on by others.

The grown-ups in your life can help you learn right from wrong.

Learning Right from Wrong

How do you know what is right? How do you know what is wrong? These are not easy questions to answer. However, looking for the answers to such questions can help you know yourself and

You were not born knowing right from wrong. You learn this as you grow. You learn by talking and listening to people you can trust. You learn by watching and copying what the people around you say and do.

As you learn right from wrong, you will make mistakes. It is okay to make mistakes. You can learn from mistakes. You can change how you do things because of your experiences.

There is a feeling inside you that helps you decide what to do. Sometimes it is called an "inner voice" or "gut feeling." Sometimes it tells you when something feels right. Other times it might say "uh-oh." Then you know something may not be right. Your inner voice can help guide you in everything you do.

A feeling inside you tells you when something seems right or wrong.

139

Sharing the Work

Sharing the work means sharing the fun.

People don't just follow laws and rules. They have responsibilities or jobs, too. By doing these jobs, they help each other and themselves.

In some families, adults and children work side by side every day, planting, tending, and harvesting crops in the fields. In other families, everyone helps sell goods in a small store or on the street.

This girl is pitching in at school by helping to water the plants.

These Guatemalan families sell fresh fruit, vegetables, and flowers on the street.

Everyone pitches in at harvest time on a German farm.

Families do different kinds of work in different places. But, in every family, grown-ups and children help one another. When everybody helps, the work gets done more quickly. And, everyone can share pride in a job well done.

Most children have jobs to do at home, too. Some take out the garbage or recycling, put away the laundry, or feed the family pet. Some children help take care of their younger brothers and sisters. Maybe you set the table or wash the dishes.

As you do your share of the family's work, you are learning to be responsible and to help others. What jobs, or responsibilities, do you have at home?

167

Appreciation of life

A conscious awareness of nature in all its aspects is a product of knowledge. With knowledge comes understanding, and with understanding comes an appreciation of the miraculous variety of nature.

Reverence for life begins when children first become aware of the wonders of the natural world. Looking through **The World of Animals** and **The World of Plants,** children will be fascinated by its diversity. They will begin to realize that humans are only one of many species that inhabit the earth. They will understand that we need to have a sense of responsibility—toward ourselves, toward our fellow human beings, and toward the animals and plants that share our planet.

Both volumes reinforce this sense of responsibility with sections about endangered animals and habitats. They also offer practical ideas for children to play their part in maintaining the delicate balance of nature.

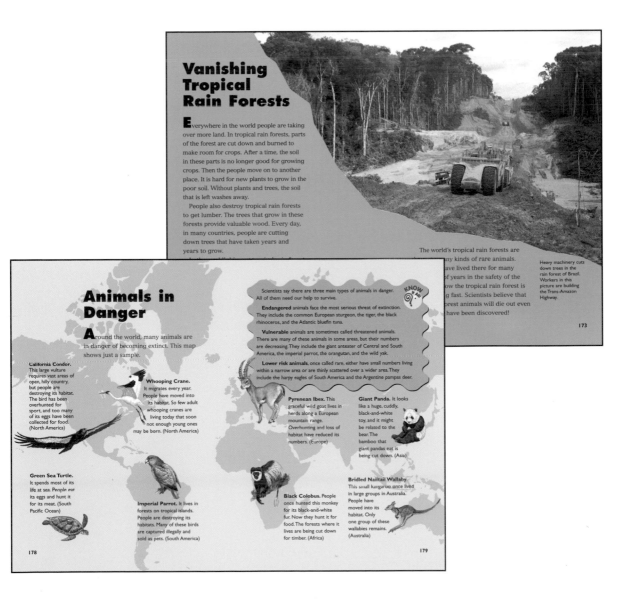

Vanishing Tropical Rain Forests

Everywhere in the world people are taking over more land. In tropical rain forests, parts of the forest are cut down and burned to make room for crops. After a time, the soil in these parts is no longer good for growing crops. Then the people move on to another place. It is hard for new plants to grow in the poor soil. Without plants and trees, the soil that is left washes away.

People also destroy tropical rain forests to get lumber. The trees that grow in these forests provide valuable wood. Every day, in many countries, people are cutting down trees that have taken years and years to grow.

The world's tropical rain forests are [...] many kinds of rare animals. [...] ave lived there for many [...] of years in the safety of the [...] ow the tropical rain forest is [...] g fast. Scientists believe that [...] orest animals will die out even [...] have been discovered!

Heavy machinery cuts down trees in the rain forest of Brazil. Workers in this picture are building the Trans-Amazon Highway.

173

Animals in Danger

Around the world, many animals are in danger of becoming extinct. This map shows just a sample.

Scientists say there are three main types of animals in danger. All of them need our help to survive.

Endangered animals face the most serious threat of extinction. They include the common European sturgeon, the tiger, the black rhinoceros, and the Atlantic bluefin tuna.

Vulnerable animals are sometimes called threatened animals. There are many of these animals in some areas, but their numbers are decreasing. They include the giant anteater of Central and South America, the imperial parrot, the orangutan, and the wild yak.

Lower risk animals, once called rare, either have small numbers living within a narrow area or are thinly scattered over a wider area. They include the harpy eagles of South America and the Argentine pampas deer.

KNOW IT ALL

California Condor. This large vulture requires vast areas of open, hilly country, but people are destroying its habitat. The bird has been overhunted for sport, and too many of its eggs have been collected for food. (North America)

Whooping Crane. It migrates every year. People have moved into its habitat. So few adult whooping cranes are living today that soon not enough young ones may be born. (North America)

Pyrenean Ibex. This graceful wild goat lives in herds along a European mountain range. Overhunting and loss of habitat have reduced its numbers. (Europe)

Giant Panda. It looks like a huge, cuddly, black-and-white toy, and it might be related to the bear. The bamboo that giant pandas eat is being cut down. (Asia)

Green Sea Turtle. It spends most of its life at sea. People eat its eggs and hunt it for its meat. (South Pacific Ocean)

Imperial Parrot. It lives in forests on tropical islands. People are destroying its habitats. Many of these birds are captured illegally and sold as pets. (South America)

Black Colobus. People once hunted this monkey for its black-and-white fur. Now they hunt it for food. The forests where it lives are being cut down for timber. (Africa)

Bridled Nailtail Wallaby. This small kangaroo once lived in large groups in Australia. People have moved into its habitat. Only one group of these wallabies remains. (Australia)

178

179

Childcraft at Home and School

In order to make the most of a child's intellectual potential, one of the most important skills that a child can acquire is the ability to think creatively. And the most crucial time when this skill should be encouraged is throughout childhood.

Every volume of **Childcraft** is full of opportunities to stimulate and encourage children to think creatively by asking the right type of questions while looking and reading.

Different kinds of questions produce different kinds of answers—and different ways of thinking are needed to find those answers. Below are explanations of some of the processes of creative thinking and some simple examples showing how **Childcraft** can stimulate these processes.

On the following pages are topic-by-topic suggestions that will help you apply these principles.

Observation

Ask questions about small details within a picture like, "What color is Peter's hat?" (**Poems and Rhymes**, page 25).

Imagining

This type of question can be asked after reading almost any selection. For example, "If you could help out in a zoo, what kind of animals would you look after?" (**The World of Animals**, pages 180-181).

Classification

Ask the child to sort objects into groups. "Which of these animals are mammals, which are reptiles, and which are birds? What other groups could you put the animals in?" (**The World of Animals**, pages 24-25).

Criticism

When looking at several examples, such as styles of architecture on pages 94-95 of **See the World**, ask which one the child likes best and why.

Interpreting

Make statements about various pictures and ask whether these statements are true or false, possible or impossible.

Making comparisons

Ask questions about people or objects in a picture. "How are the people in these pictures alike? How are they different?" (**Who We Are**, pages 10-11).

Making a summary

Using a favorite story from **Once Upon a Time**, ask the child to suggest a new title and to tell in a few words what happens in the story.

Health

Childcraft contains much information dealing with both health and safety. Children will be particularly fascinated by **About You**, which not only explains physical biology, but also examines children's emotions and social behavior.

Food for thought

Most of the food people eat comes from plants. Read about them on pages 90-105 of **The World of Plants** and pages 158-169 of **About You**.

- What type of plant is most often eaten by animals and humans?
- Can you name three different types of plants that we use for food?
- List everything you ate for lunch. What foods gave you protein? Carbohydrates? Fat?
- What substances do our bodies need very little even though we like to eat a lot of them?

What you see

How the eyes work is described on pages 70-73 of **About You**.
- Why do your pupils change sizes?
- What does it mean to be nearsighted?

Caring for yourself

Exercise is important. Pages 170-171 of **About You** explains why.
- What kinds of exercise help make your heart and lungs strong?
- What kinds build muscles?

Read about the benefits of good sleep habits on pages 176-177 of **About You.**
- What happens to someone who has not had enough sleep?
- How can you improve your sleep habits?

Your natural armor

The skin protects the body in many ways. Read about it on pages 18-21 of **About You.**
- What gives skin its color and what other function does it serve?
- What are three functions of skin?
- Which layer of skin holds your hair follicles? What else happens at this layer?

Science

The science activities in **Childcraft** are designed to encourage children to discover for themselves. The main aim is to stimulate curiosity—the same urge that prompts every scientist to experiment and investigate.

Applied science and technology

Computers are rapidly becoming part of everyday life.

◆ Read pages 106-107 of **How Things Work** with your child to find out how people use the Internet to send messages and get information.

People design and build all of the things we use today.

◆ Read about what goes into building houses on pages 152-155 of **How Does It Happen?** Help your child find and name some parts of your house or a building in your neighborhood.

Natural sciences

How do seeds become plants? Read pages 30-31 of **The World of Plants** with your child.

◆ What part of a plant grows from the seed first? What do the leaves do?

Explore the many kinds of animals.

◆ Read about kinds of animals on pages 24-25 of **The World of Animals.** Name some pets that belong in the groups.

Help your child learn how the body works. Read about bones on pages 40-43 of **About You.**

◆ What do your bones help you do?

Physical and earth science

Stars, planets, the moon, and space travel are fascinating to most children.

◆ Read pages 42-45 of **The Universe** together. Ask which story about the moon is most interesting and why.

Read pages 164-165 of **How Does It Happen?** to learn how electricity travels along wires and pages 174-175 to learn about batteries.

◆ What kinds of things run on electricity? Name some things that use batteries.

Mathematics

Learning about math is more than just learning the rules and regulations of arithmetic. Exploring **Shapes and Numbers** will reveal broader relationships among numbers, units of measurement, and processes.

Counting and shape recognition

For young children just starting to discover numbers, rhymes are an enjoyable tool to teach children to count.

◆ Read the number rhymes in **Poems and Rhymes**, pages 64-73, with your child.

Basic operations

Use **Shapes and Numbers** to help your child explore basic arithmetic.

◆ Read pages 84-85 and 98-99 with your child. Talk about some ways you use addition and subtraction in everyday life.

◆ For a child who enjoys "hands-on" learning, try pages 90-91, "You Can Add!"; 100-101, "You Can Subtract!"; and 118-119, "Square Numbers."

Measurement

Find out how we measure things.

◆ Read pages 158-159 of **Shapes and Numbers** with your child and talk about some kinds of things people measure—length, weight, and volume.

"Magic" tricks

Shapes and Numbers is filled with puzzles and games that turn arithmetic, geometry, and even the laws of chance into fun.

◆ For children who enjoy playing with numbers, try the puzzles on pages 102-103 and 104-105.

◆ Use pages 148-149, "Fun with Codes," and 150-151, "More Fun with Codes," to create and decode secret messages.

◆ For calculator fun, try the exercises on "Square Tricks" and "Magic Nines" on pages 124-125.

Math history

Pages 52-55 of **Shapes and Numbers** explain how the abacus was developed.

◆ Do the addition exercise on pages 52-53 in "Pebbles in the Sand," using some beads or dried beans. Think of other simple addition activities for your child to try.

Social studies

The main purpose of social studies is to show children how their own life experiences relate to those of other people around the world. Children come to recognize that there are more similarities than differences among people everywhere and that everyone is dependent on others for goods and services.

Clothes

Collect information about clothes from pages 70-75 of **See the World**.

- Is the statement, "People only wear clothes to keep warm" true or false? For what other reasons do people wear clothes?
- What sort of clothes would you wear if you lived in a cold, wet country? A snowy, icy country? A hot, dry country?

What are you like?

Every human being is a unique individual.

- In what ways are you different from anyone else in the world? See pages 9 and 26-27 of **About You.**
- In what ways are you similar to other people? What kinds of things do all people need wherever they live? Scan the volume **Who We Are** to find examples.

Food

Pages 44-65 of **Who We Are** describe the kinds of foods eaten in different countries. As you read the pages, ask these questions:

- How many kinds of bread can you recognize on pages 46-47?
- What is being grown on pages 48-49?
- Which animal named on pages 50-51 gives the milk you drink at home?

Homes

Read pages 80-81 of **See the World.**

- Why are some houses made of wood while others are made of clay?
- What is the primary purpose of a house?

Jobs

- How do people get things that they can't make for themselves? See pages 78-79 of **See the World.**
- How do people in families help each other? Look at pages 20-21 of **Who We Are** to find out.

Literature and language

These subjects are vitally important because language and communication are skills that are used every day. The study of language and communication falls into three parts: oral communication (speaking and listening); written communication (writing and spelling); and reading, including the appreciation of literature.

Speaking

One of the most familiar ways in which children begin to improve their speaking skills is through learning and repeating nursery rhymes. The many rhymes in **Poems and Rhymes** containing repeated words or lines are particularly useful.

- Use familiar rhymes to practice pronunciation and to teach your child to speak clearly and audibly.
- Some rhymes will be new to you. Encourage your child to learn some of them, especially if they contain new words.

Study skills

As you become familiar with the **Childcraft** volumes, you can teach your child how to use them to look up information. This skill gives children invaluable confidence when they begin using reference books for school studies.

- Start by reading the tables of contents for several volumes. Explain that each one shows the information contained in each part of that book.
- Next, choose a specific subject, such as *food*, and show your child how the index for each volume works. Note that entries for *food* appear in several volumes. The entries in **About You** will give you an opportunity to explain subentries and alphabetical order.

Listening

There's much more to listening than being able to hear. A child must learn to recognize individual words and interpret and comprehend their meaning within sentences.

- Start by reading aloud some of the shorter poems and stories from **Poems and Rhymes** and **Once Upon a Time.** Check your child's understanding by asking simple questions about each one.
- As you progress to longer and longer poems and stories, you can ask questions about the sequence of events in each tale: "What happened after . . ."

Creative activities and the arts

Every child has a natural inclination to be creative. Children often amuse themselves by making up stories, drawing pictures, making models, or playing musical instruments. Encouraging this creative urge will increase children's ability to think independently and to explore and communicate their thoughts and feelings.

Drama

Read pages 144-153 of **Art Around Us** about theater and plays.

◆ Can you name three or four kinds of work involved with creating and putting on a play besides acting?

◆ Read a short story aloud, such as *The Little Red Hen* on pages **90-92** in **Once Upon a Time**, while your child mimes the actions and facial expressions.

Music

Read about different musical instruments on pages 114-123 of **Art Around Us.**

◆ Experiment with music and sound by making the simple instruments on pages 124-127 of **Art Around Us** and playing notes and creating songs.

Painting

Learn about primary and secondary colors by doing the activity on pages 46-47 of **Art Around Us.**

◆ Look at illustrations and pictures and ask your child to point out the primary colors.

Arts and crafts

Encourage awareness of the pattern and color of everyday and natural objects.

◆ Help your child choose a paper craft project in **Art Around Us,** such as the paper-cutting activity on pages 20-21 or the weaving activity on pages 30-31, and collect the materials for it. As your child starts the project, talk about the colors your child chooses and the design or pattern your child creates.